Sounds of
Distant Drums

Sounds of Distant Drums

Alfred Sandison Hutchison

Library of Congress Control Number:		2010913293
ISBN:	Hardcover	978-1-4535-7328-0
	Softcover	978-1-4535-7327-3
	Ebook	978-1-4535-7329-7

This book was printed in the United States of America.

To order additional copies of this book, contact:
Xlibris Corporation
0-800-644-6988
www.xlibrispublishing.co.uk
orders@xlibrispublishing.co.uk
300598

Contents

Foreword

Alf Hutchison is a poet and a servant of God. No, I take that back. Alf Hutchison is a servant of God and a poet. With respect to his servitude, Alf does so with a passion and a good spirit that speaks well for his labors in God's fields of grain. When it comes time for God to reap His harvest, most of His wheat shall be found where Alf has tread with his gentle voice and calm manner.

But I am a poet, and I shall leave the spiritual aspects of the man to his Master. I shall speak to his poetry and creativity.

Alf was born with a "gift" to express himself as few others today can. He writes in the old style poetry of rhythm and rhyme of which I am so familiar and which I love with the same passion that he loves the Lord. Alf is one of the very few who can satisfy me with his verse. It reads so well that it is as if his mind and mine have the same rhythm and sounds that God so loves in his hymns and religious texts. To read his words is a pleasure. No wonder God chose him as one of his true messengers. For if you read his work, you will be drawn to his message rather than the crafting of his work. This is because, you don't have to fret or stumble over his words. I cannot tell you how he does it and neither can he. Such things are not for men to know. God knows the mind of a man and when He gives a poet a "gift", it is enough that he repeat God's message. Poetry, in the old style of rhythm and rhyme is filled with God's Truth, God's Love, and God's Beauty. What more do you need to read and hear in this world. This book is Alf Hutchison at his finest and that means your reading feast shall contain all these treasures you find in such great poetry. And all those you shall enjoy in eternal life.

Greenwolfe 1962

I dedicate this book to my loving wife Lesley Ann.

My Wife, My Friend

Hearken to the ocean, sit and listen to its roar,
Ten billion waves have broken upon its sandy shore,
Gaze upon that sunset, fiery colors of delight,
Our blessed days fast fading into inky, inky night,

Together now nere fifty years, Lesley my precious wife,
My confidante, my sole mate ... indeed my very life
Amongst a symphony of stars in that starry, starry sky,
Numbering all the days, which now have passed us by.

So young and so beautiful, when first I laid eyes on you
You have been a loving wife to me; so loyal and so true,
You are everything to me, my one true loving friend,
And I shall love you always ... a love which has no end.

Alf

Sounds Of Distant Drums

Those African nights so dark and still,
Star blazoned skies; a cricket's shrill,
Smoke spiraling heavenward from the pyre,
Hands facing palm wards towards the fire ...

Eyes transfixed on dancing embers,
Rhodesia is gone, but who remembers,
Scattered all now, around the globe,
Experiencing some, the pains of Job.

Africans angry, their bowels enraged,
Roaring like lions, heinously caged,
Answering the sounds of a distant drum;
Changes in Africa were now just begun

Memories fond, bring a tear to my eye,
Bygone 'super' days, now passed me by,
Giving our all for the green and white,
We were trained to kill; trained to fight,

Too many Rhodesians died in vain,
Many still bear the scars, the pain,
We sit now around our fires with chums
Reminiscing the sounds of distant drums ...

To the memory of Frank Du Toit, my army buddie,
and all the brave Rhodesians who gave their lives selflessly.

**AT THE GOING DOWN OF THE SUN,
AND IN THE MORNING …
WE SHALL REMEMBER THEM.**

Fiona 2010

Cowboys don't cry

My old and dear friend Frank Du Toit always used to remind me "Alf, cowboys don't cry … not in front of their horses anyway".

Well, we had just disembarked from the 'chopper' after a sortie into Mozambique; a police Land Rover had been blown to smithereens by some cowardly 'Boegs' at Kanyemba. The mood back at base camp was pretty somber; suddenly I remembered that one of our 5th Battalion blokes had brought his bagpipes.

After a few words in the chopper pilot's ear he was again airborne; this time with our lone Piper. The pilot was the best, as all Rhodesian pilots were, and he dropped our Piper on top of 'Cleopatra's needle', a huge needle like natural granite monolith towering many, many meters above the beautiful autumn leaves of the M'sasa trees. The helicopter was silent a few meters from us as the Pilot came to join the entire compliment of soldiers to witness the spectacle from our hilltop base.

As the sun touched the horizon, silhouetting our lone Piper (about a kilometer away), the haunting melody of Amazing Grace drifted across the entire valley on the cool evening breeze.

I have just returned from the Edinburgh Tattoo, August 2006, and the lone Piper there was unbelievably brilliant, but he couldn't hold a candle to our Piper; on that unforgettable eventide he played magnificently. If cowboys don't cry, as Frank insisted, I can tell you for certain that battle weary Rhodesian soldiers do; even in front of their horses.

My very dear friend Frank died on his farm in Raffengora some time ago, but I will remember that day we shared with that piper as long as I live; the day when we wept openly for all the friends we had lost; for a country we loved; for a war we believed in, but which tore us apart inside …

Tribute to Lieutenant Colonel Ron Reid-Daly
Founder of the Selous Scouts.

Gone

Gone the iconic Baobab, M'sasa, Mopani,
Gone too Zambezi, Limpopo, Hunyani,
Gone valiant soldiers with flag staffs a flight,
Gone now cherished flag of green and of white,
Gone beloved friends; silhouettes in the Sun,
Gone now Colonel Ron, Scout's warrior icon,
Gone perchance to promised place of no tears,
Gone to beat weapons ... into peaceful plow shears
Alf Hutchison

A Lion Roars

Come with me, hold tight my hand,
Whilst I show you my beloved land,
Africa's blood washes through my veins,
From Bushveld glades to savanna plains.

Have you ever heard a lion roar?
Been close enough to touch his paw,
Stared eye to eye, smelled his breath,
Observed razor teeth of instant death,

And then that roar ... that numbing sound
Sending tremors through the very ground.
A lightening swipe of five sharp claws;
No video this, you can't press pause.

Reality life, your minutes numbered,
Certain death ... your life encumbered;
But that day twas not meant to be,
God's heaven had no need of me.

A shot rang out ... a sound so sweet,
The king of beasts lay at my feet,
This was no trophy, no great prize.
My life, his death ... no compromise.

A Mother's Thoughts

What thoughts that day ... went through your mind?
Sweet gentle lady; born one of a kind,
Unique child of God, unlike non other;
Virgin birthed Christ; His earthly mother.

Within you the mysteries, of God did unwind;
What thoughts that day ... went through your mind?
Nurturer, teacher; devotedly humble;
Attending God's will; never a grumble.

Unmercifully beaten, and heinously whipped,
In His own blood, on the stone way He slipped
What thoughts that day ... went through your mind?
Man's inhumanity to man; so cruel and so blind.

A sun-darkened day; a global earthquake,
Hearts all atremble; from graves dead awake,
God's crucified Son; pierced, lifeless you find,
What thoughts that day ... Went through your mind?

What motherly thoughts ... Went through your mind?

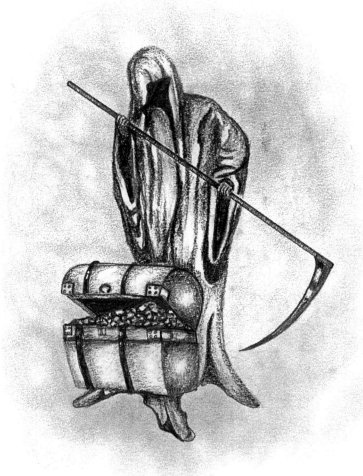

Fiona 2010

A Rich Man

A rich man told me just before he died,
And I've no reason to think he lied,
Of ships he'd sailed the seven seas,
And flying fish on salty breeze,

To commoners he gave no tithe,
This world was his alone to scythe;
And scythe he did from dusk till dawn;
His laborers broken, bent and torn;

With nose held high he tarried forth,
His countenance full of his self worth;
Then came the reaper to his deaths door,
"I've come that I may settle the score"

And the reaper did of that I'm sure,
Ceasing his evil for ever more;
No more time for his lucre to swell,
For he dwells now alone in the depths of Hell

A Time

A time of tribulation great,
Is coming to this world;
A time of war and horror,
To man will be unfurled.

A time given to make peace,
As men, man to man;
A time that mere men forfeited,
Opting war's expedient plan.

A time draws near in Israel,
Of war with Iran;
A time now heralds Lucifer,
His holy war to fan.

A time we, not too long ago,
Fought wars to end all wars;
A time of final war now looms;
Damnation, sinful cause.

A time, times and half a time,
Daniel saw in a vision,
A Time, three years and a half,
And Jerusalem's division.

A time is here, with us now,
Too late to turn around,
A time that Prophets talked about,
Forsaking hallowed ground.

A time, when fallen men look back
Upon their sinful past;
A time when mankind will recall,
Babylonian nuclear blast.

A Vulture Flies

A vulture flies on Azure blue Skies,
Africa's 'Cordon Blue' of flesh demise;
Whilst relentless sun heats up the land,
Wing feathers now by thermals fanned,

Lifting him ever higher and higher,
Beyond cloud base his prime desire;
Up to freezing heights of air so rare,
Wings outstretched ... just circling there.

With a keenly eye he surveys the land,
African savannah, picturesquely grand,
This insatiable bird in all its substance,
Seeking carrion waste in great abundance,

Predator Lions now have left their kill,
Hyenas and Jackal, eaten well their fill,
All seek shelter from the broiling sun,
Whilst scavengers supreme ... land one by one.

Abortion

At the moment of conception,
A brand new life is sown,
The seedlings of an unborn child
Within that womb are grown,

New life is very sacred,
We have no right to take
That embryo from it's haven,
For our great God has spake.

"Thou shalt not commit murder"
Moses wrote His words in stone,
That fledgling soul cannot fight back,
Defenseless, harmless, and alone.

A time will come, there is no doubt,
When you stand before the Lord;
On judgment day you cannot hide,
The wrath of God's great sword.

Do not harm unborn children,
You will pay then for your sin,
When you begged for that small life,
To be murdered from within.

African Missionary

I am a wanderer in this nomadic land,
To whom can I lend a helping hand,
To make dark lives a little lighter,
Be a bastion of peace; not a fighter.

This Darkest African, void of light.
Transient Nomads constantly fight.
Forsaken by God it appears to be;
Africa is not the land of the free.

Never shall I pass this way again,
Witness sadness, poverty and pain,
Man's blatant inhumanity to man,
Let me be of help now … whilst I can.

African Pirates

Freedom fighter or terrorist? Depends whose side you're on,
Africa's 'freedom fighters' ... proud pirates everyone,
No freedom was ever gained for Black folk's kith or kin,
Their fight was not for liberty, but to loot now from within.

Robert Gabriel Mugabe, Africa's pirate supreme,
Thieving and plundering are his passions it would seem;
But in this act he's not alone, for Grace is worse by far,
They aught now both to be rolled, in feathers and hot tar,

Nestle buys their tainted milk from Grace's stolen farm,
But a Nestle spokesman says "We are doing you no harm"
Millions of protestors will never eat their produce again,
Tainted now forever more, by Grace's shame and pain.

Whilst pirates in Somalia, wreck havoc on high seas,
Grace Mugabe sets her sails, to tramp on whom she please,
Africa, land of black pirates, from Suez to Cape Town,
Their thirst for ill-gained riches, is truely world renown.

There is not one place in Africa, that is free of piracy,
From the great Sahara desert to the azure warm Indian Sea,
With now license to plunder, these swashbucklers everyone,
Are destined to destroy our Africa ... our paradise in the sun.

Africa's Hungry Children

Kevin Carter zoomed his camera lens, that day in '94,
A starving child in Sudan, was knocking at death's door,
One vulture and one journalist; both mere meters away,
Both with different agendas; but a dying babe their prey.

A world stood aghast and horrified, by that photo in the Times,
Starvation's morbid clock unveiled, its ticking and its chimes,
But two would reap the benefit of this poor child's demise,
Sudan much needed food and aid ... and Carter, a Pulitzer Prize.

We dare not stand in judgment; for we were never there;
Africa is an angry land; fermenting poverty and despair,
"Don't touch the sick and dying" Kevin Carter had been told;
He abandoned that poor child, as new scenes did unfold.

Plagued by haunting vivid memories, of Africa's en-rapt pain,
Those abandoned starving children, surely drove this man insane,
He observed first hand, our tragic land, we seldom comprehend;
Driving him, just three month hence ... his tormented life to end.

Lord when will the suffering cease, in Africa so sublime?
Will ever we be a land, free of hunger, strife and crime?
Will the image of Kevin's photo, open up our ailing eyes,
And open up our deaf ears ... to our hungry children's cries?

Aids Orphans

Should the young children
Suffer for our sin.
Does it not grip your trembling
Heart within,

Most folk now are hard of heart,
Oblivious of their plight,
"It's not my fault, nor can I help
It's really not my fight".

Statistics on their plight we read;
Of millions dying every year,
Dying, hungry, naked and alone.
Does mankind really care.

If all the orphaned children,
Were laid side by side;
They'd circumnavigate the globe;
A highway ten feet wide.

An Author or a Poet?

When I write my thought on paper,
Forbid that I should write free verse;
Author or Poet, what shall I be
Driver of hearse … or giver of life.

Authors writhing in anguished pain
Resurrecting rhyming verse again,
Doolittle said "I think she's got it"
"Beam me up Scotty, into the rocket"

Things are improving, it's started to gel
From now on in things have to fare well.
Balancing out, it's started to rhyme,
Poets have done this since dawning of time.

But woe is me … what can I do,
To really impress the poet in you.

Paper is canvas, soft and serene,
Snow white flesh … uniquely clean;
Untouched it waits whilst I prepare,
With eyes transfixed in poet's stare;

What juice will flow from brain to ink
What joy to bring, what odes to sing,
Contrasting words of black and pink,
When will the 'word bee' deliver it's sting.

The question I ask … are you author or poet
The words a ball … what way do you throw it;
There are many skins on the proverbial cat;
Maybe, just maybe, I've shown you that.

Battle Of Blood River

Sixty four wagons in laager; the night mist cold and bland,
These 'Boers' were merely farmers, going north in search of land.
Surrounded now by Zulus, their presence was foreboding,
Twenty thousand warriors; drumming, shouting, goading.

Laagered 'Boers' for many days, upon their knees had prayed
"Lord help us in our hour of need, for we are so afraid"
At noon they made their covenant, with Spirit, God and Son
Being hopelessly outnumbered; two score and ten to one.

First light of coming morn, the fog was slowly lifted,
The war drums crescendo, to battle cry had shifted.
'Boer' spread out upon the ground, shielded by his wagon.
They lay as executioners; this was no day for flagon.

Boer's wives were not at liberty, to fire upon the foe,
They stood beside the men, their hearts vexed full of woe.
The thunder of the muskets, the battle tempest fanned;
Flintlock barrels loaded, by females trembling hand,

Woman loaded muskets, with powder, shot and waste,
Tamping down each barrel, with calculated haste,
The noise of battle deafening, its smoke a screen of white;
Confused bewildered warriors, left the battlefield in flight.

Respite to reload muskets, to take stock of the dead,
Not one Boer was missing; they counted every head.
Now soon the killing ground, slow stream of Zulu blood
Would by the time of nightfall, be a scarlet river flood.

With sun now at its zenith, bloody battle resumed afresh.
Impi warriors advancing, human sculls adorned their flesh
Brandishing their assegais', shield, spears and their staves,
Three cannons tore into their ranks; yet still they came in waves,

When the heat of battle ended, and the smoke spiraled away,
Three thousand dead drugged warriors, on battlefield there lay.
One thousand more lay wounded, proud dignities offended
Brave Boers to their feet arose; and to Zulu wounds attended.

God had given them the victory, these farmers' kith and kin
For not one of His was lost, whom He had laagered in
He had kept them from the 'Philistines', for they all loved to pray,
And they still love and honor God ... their Victor to this day.

Blinkers

Though we turn the other cheek,
Let it never make us weak,
For the blinkers that we wear,
Are the testimonies we bear.

See man's inhumanity to man,
Then expose them while you can.
Are you righteous or a sinner?
Let not evil be the winner.

Most today have tunnel vision,
'Involve me not', their firm decision,
'It's not my fault, I do not care'
'I'm not thieving silverware'

Please do not let evil prevail,
From your eyes now take the veil,
Stand your ground and boldly fight,
Fight against evil ... with all your might

Fiona 2010

Clock Of Ages

The clay beneath her muddy feet,
welled up between her toes,
A squeal of unencumbered bliss,
from her young soul arose.
Dancing in the rain alone,
arms spread-eagled wide,
An aged mother looking on,
shook her head and sighed.
"Remember well these carefree times ...
before the clock of ages chimes".

Crown of Thorns

Acacia, crown of desert thorn.
No priceless pearls or Gold
Upon Christ's head was borne,
To Cavalry's cross I'm told.

Void of gems in shades of Tourmaline
Only blood crimson crown of red.
Twas not the richest crown ere seen,
But hideous thorns instead

Those thorns of sin stand in our place,
Representing thee and me
For ere Adam fell from Godly Grace
No thorns grew on that tree.

Do You Know My Lord?

Do you feel the pain of nails, thrust through your tender hands,
Do you feel those evil thorns, a crown twisted in bands,
The excruciating agony, of iron pierced through your feet,
The shame of being spat upon, on a Roman pebbled street,

Do you feel that wretched whip, draw blood upon your back,
Hear the scourge's mocking cries; the whip's report and crack.
Do you share His anguish, when by God He was forsaken.
Disciples all but one had fled, as His righteous life was taken.

Have you carried His cursed cross, for just a pace or two,
Have you heard His cries, His pleas, bourn down in time to you.
Have you ever wept aloud, for this price He paid for sin.
Do you believe He died for you and His Spirit dwells within.

If your heart, spirit, mind and soul, have never felt His sword,
Then without doubt my friend, "You know not ... my precious Lord"

Evolution

What manner of man thinks this world was created
By an omnipotent, omniscient, all loving God?
What manner of man thinks this world *not* created?
By an omnipotent, omnipresent, all powerful God?

To think for one moment, we evolved from an Ape,
That a mouse was once, some elephantine shape,
And these in their turn, over millions of years,
Evolved from amoeba, brings me close to tears.

What is the correct order, first chickens or eggs?
Did they fly or they grope, on half evolved legs,
Was the first chicken born legless and blind?
Awaiting evolution to make up its mind.

Wise but ridiculous, foolish blind men,
You swallow their lies again and again.
Evolution is theory, not one scrap of fact,
No hard evidence, by this theory is backed.

Satan is conning men, I do presuppose,
For out of this theory, his religion arose,
He blinds humanity, to a true God creation,
Replacing God's work with absurd speculation.

The proton, the atom, and our magnetic force;
Did they come into being as a matter of course?
God's creation has precise order and symmetry,
Woven into all things; from here to infinity.

Evolutionists believe we all came by chance,
One legged people in a two legged dance,
Slow to develop in some primeval soup;
Darwinians have flown their proverbial coup!!

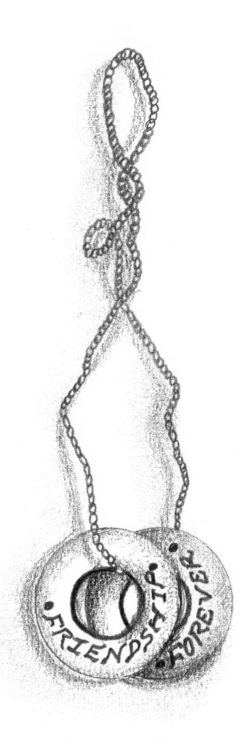

Friendship

To whom do you turn when sad and forlorn?
To a friend and thank the day she was born,
For she'll listen to you, and she'll understand
And in no time at all, your sad world seems grand.
Friendships are precious so guard them with care
That special someone whose secrets you share;
Friendships are fashioned in Heaven above,
For faith in a friend ... is the ultimate love.

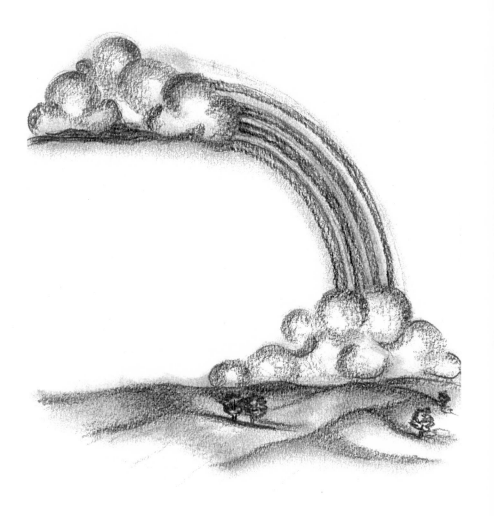

God's Promise

God's promise in His rainbow,
To Noah eons past,
Is echoed down the ages,
Throughout His world so vast.

God speaks to us through His Word;
And nature in strange ways,
Entreating us to do one thing,
"Just give to Me your praise".

What you have, He can remove,
In the twinkling of an eye;
He can bless you if He wishes;
Choose how you live or die.

He blessed Noah and his family,
Cursing those who refused to know,
To a sinful world He leaves a sign,
Timeless wisdom ... in His rainbow

Fiona

Haast's Eagle

Majestic he mounts the thermals high,
Serenely sailing yon clear blue sky;
Alone he circles, wings abreast,
Far above, his mountain nest.

Wingspan measuring thirty hands,
Soaring eagle, surveys the lands,
Can there have been a grander sight;
Haast's splendent raptor in full flight?

Alas man has robbed us of this thrill,
For sport he sought this bird to kill,
For feathers fine to adorn his head,
Birds, a thousand, lay cold and dead.

World's largest raptor in days of yore,
Haast's eagle extinct; flies no more.
Mankind forever robbed of its cry;
Forever gone from Zealand's sky

Another notch in mankind's gun,
Just killing in the name of fun.
See how men from every nation,
Make mockery of God's creation.

A time is coming, and coming fast,
When all wildlife will breathe its last;
God's creatures we have failed to feed,
Forsaking creation … in the name of greed.

Have you seen?

Have you seen a dead man talking;
Witnessed yet, a lame man walking,
A man with blind eyes sees again,
A leprous man ... now void of pain.

Have you seen water turned to wine,
Witnessed demons cast into swine;
Young girls raised now from the dead,
A mother cured ... on her death bed.

Have you seen Him walk on water,
Feed nine thousand and not falter,
Stopping a storm with one raised hand,
Restoring sight with spit and sand,

Have you seen Him nailed to a cross,
Mankind's gain, but Satan's loss,
He bled and died for you and me,
Bearing the sins of humanity;

Have you seen my precious Lord,
Holding fast salvations sword;
Beckoning you "Come trust in Me,
From this time until ... eternity"

Have you seen ... Jesus my Lord?

I must try haiku,

I must try haiku,
There is nothing left to do,
Try out something new,

Have I got it now?
Should I not include a cow?
I think not somehow.

This will take some time,
I'm committing haiku crime,
Not a verse should rhyme

So I'll start again
And from rhyming I'll refrain
Feeling quite inane

Doolittle said it thus
By George I think I've got it,
Con-que-ring hai-ku

See the setting sun,
Reflect gold upon the sea,
Clouds hold dazzling hue.

Job 22; 21

Commit to memory, that sacrosanct verse,
Job pens in his book, concise and quite clearly.
Spirit filled words, so succinct and so terse,
God's inspired words to be treated more dearly,
"Receive, I pray thee, the law from His mouth",
Now misquoting His Word, we need never fear,
Commit it to memory; Job's message is clear,
So listen to Job; wise, humble and smart
"And lay up His words in thine heart"

It was on the last leg from Kariba to Salisbury on the 3rd of September 1978 that Air Rhodesia Flight RH825 sent a Mayday call. The aircraft **"The Hunyani"** with fifty two passengers and four crew members on board was hit by a heat seeking Sam 7 missile. It had been fired by ZIPRA men ... terrorists, guerrillas, combatants, comrades, cadres, freedom fighters, soldiers (depending on your viewpoint) 18 survived the crash but later the callous murderers shot and bludgeoned 10 ... one man, seven women and two young female children. Only 8 survived to tell of the horror they had witnessed.

Lest We Forget Hunyani

He lay in hiding like a snake in the grass,
Black mamba, deadly, loathsome and crass,
Waiting in ambush, his expression quite bland;
Russian Sam seven clutched tight in his hand.

Kariba's Air Rhodesia, flight eight-two-five,
Passed overhead, but would never arrive.
Now homeward bound, merely minutes in flight,
Caught in the eyepiece of his missile's rear sight.

One Sam seven missile struck like lightening,
Mayhem on board was horrendously frightening.
Downed in the name of freedom's dark cause,
Cadre, 'freedom fighters' ... Satan's fine whores,

Twas a miracle that eighteen would even survive,
But sadly only eight would arrive home alive,
Eight surviving adults now fell dead to the floor,
Butchered by savages all thirsting for gore.

Followed by two children, aged eleven and four,
Bludgeoned by Blacks "Just to even the score"
"For stealing our land" one Black comrade said,
"We shall not stop killing, until all Whites are dead"

To the memory of passengers, pilot and crew,
To the survivors who battled to start life a new,
Like Rev. John da Costa, let us never forget,
Upon all brave Rhodesians may the sun never set.

Rhodesia ... birthplace of my heart and my soul,
Its destruction was ZIPRA's ultimate goal;
So September the third of Seventy Eight,
Remember 'Hunyani' ... and its heinous fate.

Air Rhodesia Flight RH827 Viscount "Umniati" YP-YND Shot down February
12th 1979 …There were no Survivors

Last flight of the Umniati

The Umniati Viscount will fly no more,
Like Hunyani her sister, now lost to the war,
Russian Sam sevens, operated by scum,
All fifty nine lives lost; and no battle won.

"Civilians too, must pay for our cause,
It's not only soldiers who die in the wars"
These were the words on Satan's black lips,
Aiming the heat seeking silicon chips.

Security Force members first at the scene,
Completely sickened by the carnage obscene.
Scattered remains of those precious lives,
Sisters and brothers, husbands and wives.

SAS operations were swift and precise,
Squeezing the terrorists in the jaws of their vice,
Elite airborne soldiers come to settle the score,
Satan's crass terrorist would kill no more.

This was Rhodesia's own 'Nine Eleven',
Heinously foul, by a rocket Sam seven.
No condemnation from UN world power,
No worldwide protest, in our darkest hour.

Let us never forget those left behind,
Mourning our beloved who suffered and died,
The SAS team who were put to the test,
Delivered justice for the murders, so grotesque.

How will we ever make sense of it all,
Rhodesia to Zimbabwe, it's rise and it's fall,
Too many have sacrificed life's ultimate price,
One bowl of gold nuggets, for one bowl of rice.

Both poems included in Keith Nell's book Viscount down

Lonely

No-one now to share your dreams,
To walk beside those mountain streams,
To hold your ailing, trembling hand,
To write sweet nothings in the sand;

No-one to whisper "I love you",
To keep you warm the winter through,
To share with you first buds of spring,
To show their love in a wedding ring.

No-one at home for you to say,
"I missed you my love, at work today"
To sit together at evening meal,
To tell each other just how you feel,

No-one there to forgive you gladly,
All those times you behaved so badly,
To visit your own sweet secret place,
Suspended somewhere in time and space.

No-one knows how much you cared,
Just you two and the time you shared,
Memories now left of bygone years,
The good times, bad, and all the tears.

No-one realizes just how lonely,
When 'we two' ... becomes 'me only',
God loans us soul mates, for a fleeting while,
Through His loving Grace ... once again we'll smile.

Master Jack

Master Jack was old and grey; time had passed him by,
Wizened hands betrayed his age, but a glint lay in his eye;
Physique so very frail now, had fought a thousand 'wars',
Waiting now upon God's will; Jack's life had lost its cause.

The souls of those who'd mattered; were now long in their graves,
Fond memories of times gone by, crashed over him in waves.
His children had all forsaken him; forsaken him, every one;
Embarrassed by his manner, and the sharpness of his tongue,

Tears fell upon his trembling hands, as he gazed on them with love,
These hands had been God's gift to him, from heaven up above;
Hands that blessed the Lord almighty; gave thanks for all their food,
Those hands had even built their home, beside the forest wood.

Hands carved their wooden furniture; and planted crops to sell,
When drought had struck the barren land, they dug for him a well,
Skilled hands had caught his children, emerging from the womb.
Seven boys, and three small girls; now adults in full bloom.

Gnarled hands from manual labor, digits enflamed and sore,
Busy hands made impotent; were functioning no more,
Spastic hands, arthritic hands; worked now 'to the bone',
Not one soul to help him farm; Master Jack prayed all alone.

"My Lord I have to thank you, for these two hands of mine,
The countless tasks accomplished, through your two gifts Divine",
Calloused hands now pressed in prayer; "I wish new turf to roam",
Soulful eyes glinted heavenward, "Please Lord … take me home"

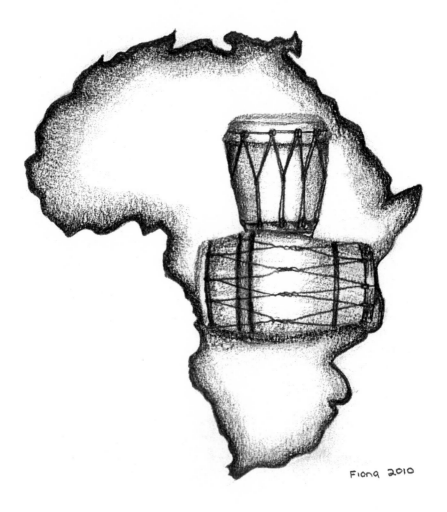

A tribute to a fellow South African poet whom I have never met

Our African Queen

With carefully chosen words she draws,
On an African canvas which she adores,
Then paints her pictures in colorful hues,
Light shades of darkness, to bluest of blues.

Compassion lies deep within her bone marrow,
For our parched land, its pain and its sorrow,
From Africa crying with its aches and pains ...
To the joy that comes, with the blessed rains.

She holds South Africa in the palm of her hand,
Passionately dedicated to God's beautiful land.
Cindy Kreiner Sera, is our poets dear name,
Seeking no glamour, neither fortune nor fame.

A poetic genius, both humble and wise,
Worthy, we all think, of a Nobel Prize.
An equal to Cindy, has yet to be seen,
Our precious poet ... our African Queen.

My Dad

"Son ... I have bad news for you,
Your father died today",
"Sorry ... we'll send you home"
Was all he had to say;

I left my soldier comrades,
On the back of an RL
In that hot Zambezi valley,
The land we knew as Hell.

Frank my friend had told me
That 'Cowboys do not cry;'
'Not in front of their horses'
Came my choking sad reply

I cried that whole trip home,
Remembering what Frank said
'Cowboys definitely do not cry'
So this soldier cried instead.

I loved my Dad so dearly,
He was never meant to die,
So many words unspoken,
And now he's gone ... but why?

So if you have a father,
Love him, make him smile,
God has only loaned him to you,
For just a fleeting while.

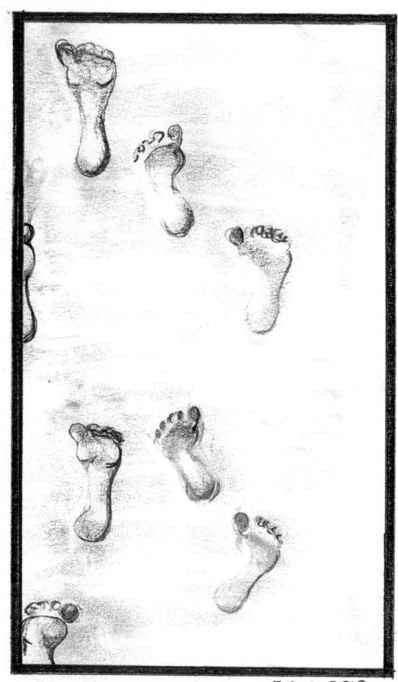

Fiona 2010

My Friend

Please walk a while with me my friend,
Along life's beach which has no end,
Beside its oceans ebbs and flow,
That special place where true friends go.

Hold my hand and watch the sea,
And wonder why all birds fly free;
Your inner soul may ask you 'why'?
Don't shed a tear, no time to cry,

For God made every grain of sand,
He made it bold, He made it grand,
He made it thus, that you and me,
Might wonder for eternity.

If I love you, and you love me,
Then surely it was destiny,
That you and I should be as one,
To sail into that setting sun.

But for the while just be my friend,
My love for you will never end;
For time will set, of that I'm sure …
Our sails towards God's heavenly shore.

Painting on Auction

She gazed on me through pale blue eyes,
Sweet lady in the frame,
Her beauty caught in a flash of time,
Fair damsel without name,

Soft lips of ripe strawberry red,
So vulnerable,so alone,
White skin pale and flawless,
Fragile as China bone;

Her trussed up golden layered hair,
Coiffured to near perfection;
Jewelry draped about her neck
A priceless pearl collection

Tears I now see in her eye,
This lass I had never met
Her haunting countenance for sure
Is one I'll nere forget.

The gavel woke me from my trance,
The auctioneer's voice so bold
"Your priceless painting,Satan,
Is now officially sold."

Life is like that work of art,
Painted in shades of leaven,
Focusing on the untold riches,
On earth and not in Heaven.

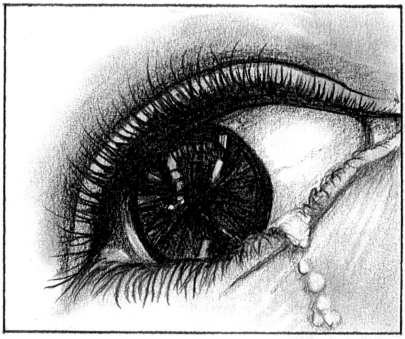

Fiona 2010

Reality

In the crowd she passed me by;
Through a land I'd never been,
Might she be a mother, a housewife?
Perhaps some beauty queen.
Her teeth were almost perfect,
White soldiers in a row,
With ruby lips to frame them;
In that land I did not know.
Those stunning eyes still haunt me,
So soft, so pale, so green,
Truly the most stunning eyes,
That I had ever seen,
Her radiant smile, freely given me,
Was etched upon my soul,
Her selfless act of kindness,
Had made my spirit whole.
Then rudely wakened from my dreams,
I faced mortality;
In a world that's forgotten how to smile
... Back to reality.

Remember 9/11?

Can you recall where you were, September nine/eleven?
When all hell did brake loose; from Kamikaze heaven,

In disbelief, you watched aghast ... another plane, another blast.

Can you recall your disbelief, when Pan Am hit those Towers?
Proud symbols to a decadent world, of capitalistic powers;

Twin phallic symbol monuments ... to green backs, dollars, cents.

Can you recall those heinous scenes; gut wrenching, grim and dire?
The New York skyline so unique, engulfed in smoke and fire,

This was no false illusion ... Pandora's Box of mass confusion,

Can you recall saying farewell, to those who died in vain?
Giving thanks to firemen; friends, you'd never see again,

Saluting unsung heroes ... with your tears of grief and woes.

Can you recall the Israeli news; so grotesquely vile and sour?
Palestinians singing in the streets; praising 'Islam's finest hour'!

Never will we be the same ... Jihadist joy, now Islam's shame.

Can you recall having pondered, before that fateful flight?
A second 'Viet Nam' would rage; with not an end in sight

Times have changed now in The West ... Jihad won't let free man rest.

Can you recall when on your knees, praising God through prayer and song,
Protect our nation, even though, in the eyes of God, we have gone wrong,

A Savior stands now in the wings ... He is Lord of lords and King of kings.
Choose now America, Hell or Heaven ...
or have you all forgotten ... nine/eleven?

**To the memory of the Rhodesian Helicopter Pilots and
the 20mm cannon Gunner. Two men one helicopter;
known as K-car ... Killer-car.
A formidable force in the Rhodesian Bush War.**

Rhodesian K-Car

Chopper' pilot calmness, Cannon gunner's skill,
Two minds in perfect harmony, Flew in now for the kill,
Ten comrades in arms, Pinned down by enemy fire,
Ambushed and compromised, their backs now to the wire.

One pilot and one gunner, men who knew no fear,
S.O.S. came through to them, urgent ... but so clear,
"K-car, Call sign Bravo, Contact, Contact, Contact"!
Pilot with nerves of steel, and veraciously exact,

"We have you visual, four o'clock", crackled in the pilot's ear
He responded calmly "Roger call sign Bravo ... illuminate a flare"
Flare lit up and in they flew, oblivious of the danger;
Twas deaths turn to roll the dice, with life their coin of wager.

Two hands upon the cannon grips, one finger on the trigger,
Gunner's eye took a site, through peep site to the jigger;
Bullets ripped into the cockpit, of that killer-car machine,
Barely two year out of school, K-car gunner ... aged nineteen

Fire Force airborne pilot, turned cannon to the smoke,
Gunner pressed the trigger, and the dragon now awoke;
Twenty millimeter cannon, boomed forth volcanic life
Spewing deadly rounds, of instant death and strife.

No place for enemy to hide, from this matchless opponent;
Terrorists now in full flight, were gunned down in a moment.
The Kill-car hovered overhead, just six foot off the ground,
Two enemy lay screaming, but from thirty dead ... no sound.

Most men of war, whom I knew then, have turned now to the Lord,
They have turned into plow shears, their weapons and their sword.
Lord please teach us here in Africa, love for one another;
Take xenophobic intolerance from us, teach us to love our brother.

Salute to 'Author unknown'

"Is it not strange, that princes and kings,
And clowns who frolic in circus rings,
And common folk like thee and me,
Are builders for eternity"?

"To each is given a book of rules,
A block of stone and a bag of tools,
And each must make ere time has flown
A stumbling block or a stepping stone".

Unknown is the author of this fine thesis,
But it's wisdom therein never ceases
My salute to you poet friend unknown,
For by these words, through life I've grown.

Alf Hutchison and Author unknown

Soldier

He held Dads medals in his hand,
As they lowered his casket down
A hole dug in that barren land,
On the slopes of Salisbury Town.

Head bowed down towards the sand,
Tears raining from his eye,
On the Medals clutched within his hand,
Like raindrops from on high.

He listened to the prayers and Word,
And to the eulogy;
No finer words had this lad heard,
Of his only progeny.

Rhodesia was, in those first days,
Untamed and fancy free,
Dingaan was the black mans praise,
King of M'tabele.

All the pacts and treaties broken,
By Dingaan and his son,
Treaties both penned and spoken,
Now broken every one.

Rebellion grew against those white
By blacks a thirst for war,
Warriors vexing their great might
Were fifty score, times four.

An assegai had pierced his chest,
As he fought hand to hand.
These 'Murungus' coming from the west,
Unwelcomed in Black's land.

Proud medals from some distant war,
His life's worth left to show,
Reminders of campaigns of yore,
Fought for a land … he'd never know.

Fiona 2010

Something wrong

Forgive me; did I say something wrong,
Your countenance has changed; no smile.
Pushed to a depth, I don't belong.
Your plaything, for just a fleeting while.
Long gone, your voice of lovebird song;
When you would go that extra mile
Was I born to be your sounding gong,
Rasping at my inner soul, metal to a file.
Why did it end; did I do something wrong.

Fiona 2010

Sounds of South African Drums

Do you hear those drums my boy, asked a father of his son,
They are the drums of Chaka, gathering each and every one;
Hear those xenophobic drums, beating deep within your soul;
Beating for us blacks, umfaan, for foreigner's bell to toll.

They are beating for us blacks, my son, to answer to the call.
It is time for all the foreigners, either bold or great or small,
To finally pay the price, for the 'evil' they have done,
Neither shall we rest at night ... until there is not one.

No, not one of them left alive, in our ancestral land,
Their blood flows warm and crimson, like Kalahari sand.
We have no care for others, nor matter what they think,
We have to rid our hallowed land of their repugnant stink.

Foreigners took from us a bitter land, to turn it into honey,
They took from us our bartering; introduced us to their money.
Doctors healed us with their medicines; but not Sangomos way
They preached of one called Jesus Christ ... to Him we aught to pray

They made a vow upon this soil; they will not turn a sod,
Until they have built a church, to honor their great God,
Their God is not ancestral ... we mock, He has no power;
Fetch my assegai, and my shield: its now their final hour.

Our ancestral god 'nkosi', by Sangomos we are told,
Made us fearless warriors, steadfast, strong and bold
So fetch my faithful spear umfaan, dip it in the blood,
Time to wipe out all of them; White chewers of the cud.

Bulala! Bulala! Kill them every man, his wife and child;
Kill, kill my ebony son, the strong, the meek and mild.
Hold well your spear and your shield, hold them high aloft,
Fill your empty spirit son, upon the blood we've quaffed.

Then our ancestral god 'nkosi' ... at the setting of life's sun,
Will reward us for each foreigner; having left alive not one.
We then shall bask and hunt again, with bow, stone axe and club,
Whilst the 'evil' the foreigners brought ... returns to virgin scrub.

The Greatest Love Story Ever Told.

He died for you, He died for me,
He died for His friends on Calvary.

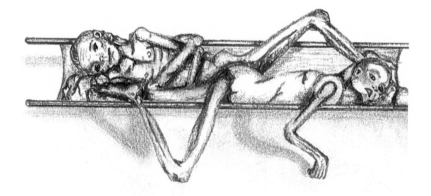

AS SEEN THROUGH THE EYES OF A MEMBER OF THE FORCES,
WHO LIBERATED THE SITES OF THE HOLOCAUST

The Holocaust

The rain how it fell; the cadaver smell,
My eyes transfixed on that pit of Hell;
Vapid flesh foul, horrendously bland.
But why this carnage, I don't understand;

Retching, gagging, holding back the bile.
I turn from the evil to rest for a while,
From decomposing mothers, fathers and child;
Satan's work, merciless, callously wild.

Laid out in graves grotesquely remorse,
Lucifer's carnage has taken its course
In a dance of death, contorted and thin,
Thousands of bodies, bound together by skin.

Now sixty years passed, will I ever forget.
That day when in person, with Satan I met;
He showed me firsthand his evil, his sin.
Flames of contempt still burn deep within.

Wise men instruct us 'we must never, forget',
'Upon the memory of them, let the sun never set';
For six million Jews paid the ultimate cost,
I know, I was there, at the great Holocaust.

The Lone Piper

Alone upon a hilltop, stood a piper boldly grand,
A soldier far away from home; Scotland his homeland.
Sunset now behind him, a lonely silhouette,
Hands upon the chanter, so passionately set.

The finest of the finest, the pride of Scotland's best,
Black Watch Regimental medals, blazoned upon his chest,
Hot sun, not a hint of breeze, to sway his pleated kilt.
His stoic comrade's passion, would never ever wilt.

Troops standing at attention, in the valley far below,
Heard the haunting melody, as the tune began to flow.
"Amazing Grace how sweet the sound that saved a wretch like me,
I once was lost but now am found, was blind but now I see"

In perfect rank and file they stood, firearms reversed and still.
Lamenting sound filled the air, pipes melancholy shrill.
That Piper in the dying light, piped as nere before,
Haunting melody of pipes, brought shivers to the core.

Proud Scots, courageous men, true soldiers one and all,
Called to war by their King, they answered to the call.
They had come to honor heroes, those who'd lost their lives,
Men who'd left behind parents, children, wives;

Tears welling in the eyes, of those courageous men.
When would the next man die? not who, or why … but when.

The Truth

Men worship political correctness; true curse of Babylon,
Accepting all religions now, lest it offends someone,
Lord they have blasphemed, the true meanings of Your word,
Scriptures have been altered, to mean things quite absurd,

They teach there is no sin now; no-one has gone astray,
And there is no need for Jesus, a ransom price to pay.
Man now says that Genesis, is only just a myth,
That You never created animals, on the day of the fifth.

Bold preachers are a rarity, who would die preaching the cross,
Instead we have false teachers, babbling heresies and dross;
The gospel of Christ crucified, they now no longer tell,
Why should there be a savior; for there in no fiery Hell.

Devine and Holy Scripture, would in latter days be mocked,
The foundations of Your Church, would be unfathomably rocked,
We are inundated with new courses, and secular books to read,
Few now savor your divine word, and its truths therein to heed.

But Jesus Christ upon that cross; He bled and died for me,
MY Free gift of grace from God; Sacrificed on Calvary,
He suffered hanging there; my sins upon his shoulders,
Plus the sins of all mankind; the weight of a million boulders.

He saved me on that fateful day, from eternal life in Hell,
I am now saved from damnation, and I can witness well,
Of Someone who loved me so; He would even die for me,
My Jesus Christ and my Lord; Sacrificed to set men free.

The truth is that same Jesus Christ; Who suffered death upon a tree,
God resurrected from the grave ... and now ... He's coming back for me.

The wings of an eagle

Lord give me the wings of an eagle,
Allow me to soar upon high.
Lord give me the wings of an eagle,
Allow me to float in Your sky.
Lord give me the wings of an eagle,
Allow me your Rapture on high.

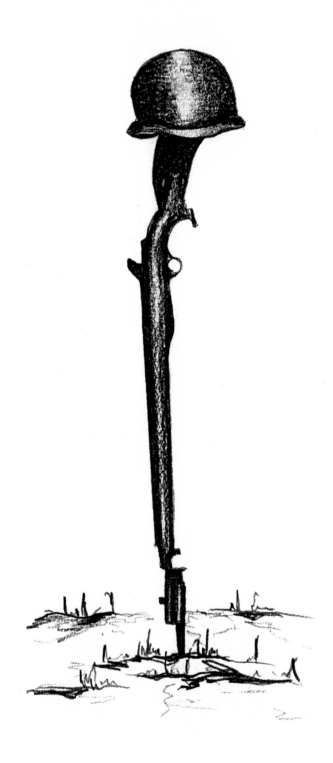

At the going down of the sun,
And in the morning ... we will remember them

Unknown Soldier

"Where have all the soldiers gone,
Gone to graveyards everyone;"
Peter Seeger's sung melodies,
A grieving mother's sad memories.
Our mother's sons gone to war,
Repeated untold times before,
Gone to fight for kith and kin,
Each mother's heart broken within.
Waiting for that 'gram' to arrive,
Your son is not coming home alive.
Your son is missing presumed dead,
That is how those grams were read.
Now buried away, so far from home
Beneath some foreign turf and loam.
A Bayoneted rifle marks the hamlet,
Atop the rifle, a mangled helmet,
No 'dog tags', neck laced identity,
An unmarked grave ... for eternity.

Where is the sanity of it all,
Where is the sense of it all,
"When will we ever learn,
When ... will we ever learn."
Alf Hutchison

What if?

What if we were incapable of love?
Or to see the beauty in a snow white dove,
What if this life simply held no joy,
No playful shenanigans of a baby boy,
What if in this life we had no peace?
Just a greed to own the Golden Fleece;
What if mankind harbored only blindness,
No long-suffering and zero kindness;
What if we just lived and died,
Were never truthful, but always lied.
What if in this life there was no hope,
Just a scaffolding and hangman's rope
What if we possessed no goodness;
No faithfulness nor loving-kindness
What if we spent our lives in fears
Of addicts, drunks and sexual queers,
What if we had lived in the time of Lot,
God destroyed Gomorrah, but mankind forgot.
What if I tell you "Its now taking place,
This world degenerates at diabolical pace"
What if Sodom and Gomorrah returns as 'old sod',
Again man will witness ... the awesome wrath of God!!!

A tribute to those territorial troopies who fought in the bush war.
Men of the fifth Battalion, Rhodesian Regiment.

Where are the men of the fighting fifth?

Where are the men of the fighting fifth?
Prime men without fear nor shame,
Where are the men of the fighting fifth?
Their proud dying flame ... forgotten by name,

Where are the men of the fighting fifth?
Resplendent in camouflage gear,
Where are the men of the fighting fifth?
Brave warriors devoid of all fear,

Where are the men of the fighting fifth?
Some with the hearts of King Saul,
Where are the men of the fighting fifth?
Who answered the call ... and gave it their all

Where are the men of the fighting fifth?
Honored by none ... for a job well done,
Where ... please tell me where are
Rhodesia's .... men of the fighting fifth?

Sounds of Zimbabwean Drums

The drums are calling you old man, and grow louder by the day.
They are calling you to judgment, it's now your time to pay,
For the wrongs you've done Zimbabwe, the trust which you betrayed.
So hear those drums a pounding, hear well, and be afraid!

The drums are calling you old man, and grow louder by the day.
For The cries of those you murdered, simply will not pass away,
In a land we called Rhodesia, Twas truly 'God's own land',
You trashed it with your gluttony and evil thieving hand.

The drums are calling you old man, and grow louder by the day,
You starved your kinfolk of their food; the meek, your favored prey,
With all your years of tyranny and lavish trips abroad.
Their proud heritage you squandered, through patronage and fraud.

The drums are calling you old man; and grow louder by the day
For your fellow brothers in Africa, are now ashamed to say.
That Cholera, poverty and starvation, are the heritage you've left.
But help won't come from cowardly Africa; it will come now from the West.

The drums are calling you old man, and grow louder by the day;
Twas not the world that brought you down, but Christians who could pray.
God heard the prayers of His saints to stop you in your pride,
The gates of hell, I believe, are broad and high and wide

The drums are calling you old man, and grow louder by the day,
The drums have sound their verdict; listen well to what they say,
For they foretell of your demise, and they have much to tell.
So hear the drums, old man, and listen to them well.

The drums are calling you old man, and grow louder by the day
Your 'war vets' will abandon you, to flee another way
Now listen to those drums old man their message is not vague
They are pounding out across the world "We'll see you in the Hague!!"
By Alf Hutchison inspired by an unnamed e mail

Lightning Source UK Ltd.
Milton Keynes UK
UKOW051133110112

185162UK00001B/377/P